My Daddy Has a Brain Cold

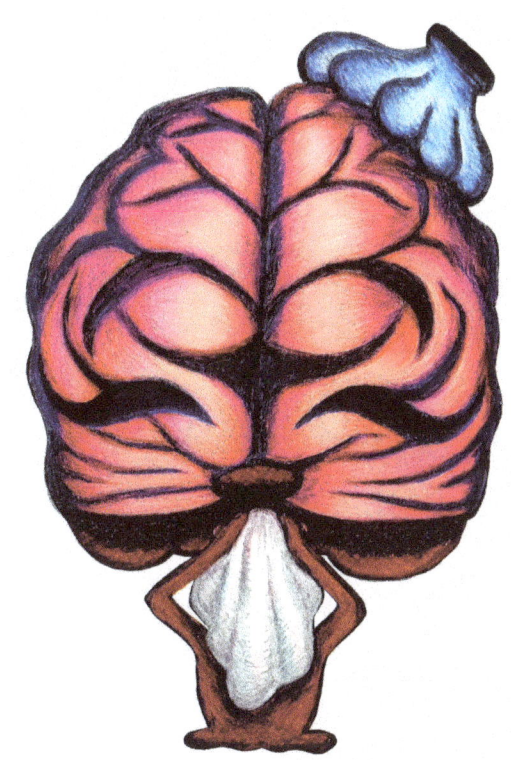

ISBN 979-8-89309-296-7 (Paperback)
ISBN 979-8-89309-298-1 (Hardcover)
ISBN 979-8-89309-297-4 (Digital)

Copyright © 2024 Susan Newman
All rights reserved
First Edition

Thank you, Katie George, for my title page picture.

All rights reserved. No part of this publication may be reproduced, distributed, or transmitted in any form or by any means, including photocopying, recording, or other electronic or mechanical methods without the prior written permission of the publisher. For permission requests, solicit the publisher via the address below.

Covenant Books
11661 Hwy 707
Murrells Inlet, SC 29576
www.covenantbooks.com

My Daddy Has a Brain Cold

Susan Newman

My dad is a hero. He was in the military before I was born. Then, when I came along, he stayed home to take care of me every day. I don't remember what that was like, but I see us in pictures. Also, my mom tells me stories about it. In the pictures, my dad is always holding me, holding my hand, helping me on the slide, or sharing snacks with me. I love to look at these pictures; sometimes I share the picture books with my dad too. I do remember my dad taking me to pre-K, reading to my class, and taking me to doctor appointments while my mom went to work. Then everything started to change.

One day, my dad was driving me to an appointment, and we backed into a fence post; I thought it was funny, but my mom did not.

Then I noticed that my dad was not driving much at all. Suddenly my dad stopped coming to my school to eat lunch with me and didn't want to share snacks or play with me or my brother after school. He would still meet us every day when we got off the bus, but we weren't allowed to stay home with him anymore like we did before. Instead, we had to go to my granny's house next door to play until my mom came home from work. Other things changed too. My mom started cutting the grass, fixing things around our house, running all the family errands, and taking care of all the animals we had. Dad sometimes would come out of his room wearing my mom's shirt or with his shoes and no socks!

Sometimes I think grown-ups think that we kids don't see what is going on, but my little brother and I knew things were changing. As the middle child and only girl in the family, I had to find out what was happening in our house. Finally, I asked my mom why things were different and what was happening; this is also the day that my life changed.

Mom told me that my dad has a "brain cold."

What's that? How did this happen? Will I get it too? Will my little brother or my big brother get it? What will happen to Dad now? When will he get better? I had so many questions to ask.

My mom smiled big, but I could see she was sad as she started to explain what was happening. She pulled me close as she said that my dad has something called frontotemporal dementia. This is a big word that means my dad's brain doesn't work like it did before—like it has a cold. Mom explained that it's kind of like when I have a cold that causes me to sleep a lot, lie around the house, feel grumpy, not want to eat, and sometimes say things that are not kind. I couldn't imagine my dad doing any of these things since he was always fixing something, building something, or playing with us.

He was the strongest and nicest man I knew. I've seen him dance with my mom in the kitchen while she was trying to cook. He helped me learn to be gentle when I picked up our puppy and when he taught me to feed our chickens, but soon I would see what she was talking about. I asked if giving Daddy orange juice and soup would help him feel better.

Mom said that would be very sweet and kind for us to do, but it will not make Dad's "brain cold" go away; she said that just like she helps us when we are sick, we must help Dad now.

"Will my brothers or I catch Dad's cold? What if you catch it?"

Mom hugged me close and said that Dad's brain cold is not a germ that others can get. She doesn't know why Dad got this brain cold, and there is no way to make it go away. But there are some good things about his sickness.

I didn't understand how my dad being sick could be a good thing at all, so I asked how this could be.

Mom told me that Dad doesn't understand that he is sick, that he still loves all of us, and that now that he is sick, he needs all of us to help him much more than we ever did before. Since my dad needs us more, we can spend more time with him sharing cookies, milk, and hot chocolate. We have learned to talk quietly to him and not run around his room, and no more playing on his bed with our toys. Most exciting is that sometimes my little brother and I get to have sleepovers with my Granny on school nights when Mom needs to take Dad to the doctor in another town. I miss them, but I love getting to have sleepovers!

My dad still likes to give me big hugs sometimes but doesn't like for us to be in his room or eat with him anymore. At Thanksgiving, he wasn't in his room when I went to get him for dinner, so we got to play hide-and-seek to find him. My mom won since she found him outside in his shed. He doesn't like to come out of his room very often and will sometimes hide in his bathroom if he is upset, but Mom says that we should just give him time to calm down like when we are upset; she says that sometimes Dad puts himself into time out by going into his bathroom and staying there for a long time. I like to read to him at night, even if I read through the bathroom door.

Other things are different now too. I remember when my dad would run around in the yard chasing me, push me on the swing, or go to the park with us to have picnics and play. I really loved going on long walks with him, my mom, and my brothers, but these things don't happen anymore.

My dad spends most of his time wearing his earphones and watching people build stuff or music videos on his tablet. My dad sometimes yells when he talks to the dogs (or my mom), shuts the door hard, and ignores us when we are trying to talk to him. My mom sleeps on the couch or in the guest room now too. Each night, my dad would walk our dogs, but now we help my mom do this before we go to bed. My brothers and I take turns helping my mom clean up and take out the trash since my dad used to do this too.

I'm only seven years old, but Mom says I am a big helper because I clean up my toys at night, help my little brother sometimes, and put away some of the dishes.

Sometimes I get sad and cry because I want my dad to play with me or sit by me at the table. When this happens, my mom sits close and tells me that it's okay for us to miss our time with Dad and be sad that things have changed. We make hot chocolate and color pictures that I can hang up in his bedroom later. Mom says that I can always ask questions or talk to her about Dad and how things have changed. She also told me that it's okay for me to talk to others—like my doctor, teacher, or school counselor—about his brain cold.

I told my teacher, and one day I got to share some of my dad's favorite snacks with my classroom friends. I don't really want to tell my school friends about Dad's brain cold because I don't think they would understand. My teacher hugs me tight sometimes and tells me it's okay to talk to her, and she thinks I am a strong girl for helping my dad and mom every day.

I miss my dad coming to my school for lunch and class parties. I really miss him helping with homework, playing with us, and sitting by us at dinner, but I'm glad that he still hugs us sometimes and shares snacks on some days.

I'm sad that my dad has changed because of his brain cold, but I'm excited that we can still share hot chocolate and treats on some days and really excited that I get to help him like he used to help me. I understand that my dad's brain cold will not go away, but I love that we get to take care of him and share laughs, like when he makes funny faces at my mom or sings loud with the radio! I don't know what will happen now, but I know my mom will hug us tight every day and that we will always be a family. Dad's brain cold has changed him forever, but he is still a hero to us. My mom says that now we are a whole family of heroes!

About the Author

Susan is the proud mother of three, the wife of a Navy veteran, a daughter, a sister, and an aunt. She has lived most of her life in Florida, where she enjoys beautiful beaches, rivers, and outdoor activities with her children. On weekends you can often find her and her family baking and gardening in the wonderful Florida weather. Susan is passionate about learning from others around her and loves to work with children in her community.